the Appalling Guests

Dyeing his chest hair is truly weird, but what can a serious Elvis do?

the Appalling Guests

SOCIAL STEREOTYPES FROM THE
Telegraph magazine

Victoria Mather
and
Sue Macartney-Snape

JOHN MURRAY

For
Hilary de Ferranti
always a wonderful friend
V.M.

and

For
Jean Gilbert
S.M-S.

Text © 2000, 2001, 2002 and 2003 Daily Telegraph plc
and Victoria Mather

Illustrations © 2000, 2001, 2002 and 2003 Daily Telegraph plc
and Sue Macartney-Snape

First published in 2003 by John Murray (Publishers)
A division of Hodder Headline

1 3 5 7 9 10 8 6 4 2

A CIP catalogue record for this title is available from the British Library

ISBN 0-7195-6585 5

Typeset in Monotype Bembo 11.5/15pt by
Palimpsest Book Production Limited, Polmont, Stirlingshire

Printed and bound in Spain by
Bookprint S.L., Barcelona

John Murray (Publishers)
338 Euston Road
London
NW1 3BH

Foreword

IF SOMEBODY WANTS to put pen to paper about politics, modern warfare, animal husbandry or the art of basket-weaving, it is unlikely that he or she will get the chance to do so, without demonstrating some familiarity with the subject. Yet journalists and novelists fill acres of print every day with descriptions of English social life which make howlers so gross that one imagines Mr John Prescott taking his constitutional in a minefield.

They can't spell the names of clubs. They think grouse are reared. They insist upon referring to a peer's wife as Lady Magnesia Freelove, rather than Lady Freelove. They imagine that Ascot is chic. When I edited newspapers, I pleaded with our staff that getting these things right was not a matter of snobbery, or deference to a fading aristocracy, but vital to maintaining the trust of educated readers. If we could not get the small things right, why should they believe us on the big ones?

Most social journalism is what we might call shotgun stuff. Heavy patterns are fired, of which a few pellets connect. Much of the lead disappears into the scenery.

Victoria Mather and Sue Macartney-Snape, by contrast, are Olympic riflemen. For almost a decade, they have provided a running commentary upon English upper-middle class life which displays a wit, wisdom and above all intimate familiarity, which puts all rivals to shame. They achieve for social observation what the Duke of Northumberland and Hugh van Cutsem do for shooting: they never miss.

My mother, Anne Scott-James, who provided a good deal of social observation of her own for newspapers a generation ago, remarks that any fool can write a column for a week or two, but only a very few writers are sufficiently talented to maintain the pace for years on end.

She was married to Osbert Lancaster, whose pocket cartoons displayed some of the same qualities as Sue Mac-S's watercolours today: like Osbert, Sue never gets hemlines wrong, nor fails to notice the trinkets on sitting-room tables. She captures perfectly the expression on the face of a squire which Evelyn Waugh once described as reflecting 'that sly instinct for self-preservation which passes for wisdom among the rich.'

Reading some of Victoria's gems in this latest collection, I find myself also thinking of Saki, the supreme social satirist. In any social gathering, Victoria is not merely listening intently – she never forgets a line. Her affection for the world about which she writes is never in doubt, but nor is her needle-sharp perception of its frailties and follies.

I was lucky enough to edit the *Daily Telegraph* when Mather and Macartney-Snape threw their first grenade, dished up their first soufflé, blew their first kiss – choose your own figure of speech – for our Magazine. I love and revere both in equal measure. The world they portray is today trembling amid the assault on foxhunting, the translation of regal status from the Windsors to Posh and Becks, the interminable chaos at PJs.

But they bring laughter even to a society haunted by the impending release from captivity of Jeffrey Archer. They allow us to forget for a moment that we are obliged to share our planet with Michael Douglas and Catherine Zeta-Jones. Ladies and gentlemen (Victoria is shuddering in my ear 'only hookers are "ladies"') – raise your glasses to Mather and Macartney-Snape.

Max Hastings
Spring 2003

Acknowledgements

Max Hastings is the godfather of Social Stereotypes. It is now ten years since Max sent out an edict demanding a series of caricatures for the *Daily Telegraph's* Chelsea Flower Show supplement, depicting fierce dowagers obsessed with sweet peas and brigadiers bent on mass destruction of the slug. Sarah Miller arranged the marriage between Sue and me. It seems extraordinary that we'd only met once before, now we've been together for 500 Social Stereotypes, the column that evolved from the original dowagers and brigadiers when Emma Soames became editor of the *Telegraph Magazine*. Five hundred weeks is a long time in a marriage, and it's bizarre to think that when we began there were no computer whiz-kids, or lifestyle gurus. The blonde 4x4 drivers hadn't blocked the Chelsea streets, nor had the terrifying proliferation of baby showers and book clubs swung over from the States. The Countryside Campaigner was peacefully preoccupied with hedgerows, otters and badgers, not the militant bastion between us and the Blairite destruction of our green and pleasant land. Sue and I are always being asked 'When are you going to run out of Social Stereotypes?' And the answer is never, because society is constantly reinventing itself. We would like to thank Michelle Lavery, the new editor of the *Telegraph Magazine*, and our commissioning editors over the years, Sarah Crompton, Sarah Miller, Louise Carpenter and Vicki Reid. Denis Piggott, Stereotypes production manager, is our hero. Sandie Elsden and Juliet Caulfield never fail to reassure that the column has made it – particularly when transmitted from the Safaricom mobile telephone bush in the Masai Mara.

Those who helped me with the characters within include Kathleen Baird-Murray, Janet Street-Porter, Roger Bramley (the epitome of the gentleman cyclist), James Rose, Camilla Osborne, Christopher and Philippa Chetwode and Mark and Moira Andreae (all very sound on dogs and *The Archers*). Stereotypes could not exist without my indefatigable reporters from the youth front: Johnny, Sarah and India Standing, and Caroline Wrey. It is difficult for a Very Busy Woman to decide who is more supportive to her in her life, her husband or her hairdresser. My husband, John Raymond, is a star, but without John Barrett I would never have discovered the Pedicure Addict. When I was homeless due to having the builders, Sue and Douglas Gordon took me and the Pekingese in and made sure Stereotypes continued from their kitchen table.

It is a joy to be published by John Murray. John himself, Caroline Knox and Caroline Westmore never fail to make us feel cherished.

Victoria Mather
Hampshire, 2003

Anthony and Amanda assume domestic fairies are going to load the dishwasher

The Appalling Guests

ANTHONY AND AMANDA were going to the Hotel du Cap, but Ant's bonus wasn't quite up to snuff so they've descended on the Fortescues instead. The implication, as they tuck into Charlie Fortescue's champagne on Friday night, is that the Fortescues should be honoured. 'How is life in dozy old Somerset, eh? Amanda and I are always in the Med at this time of year but, frankly, the other people are so trashy now we thought we'd give it a miss. Mind you, it takes less time getting to Nice than driving down here. Don't know how you stand those funny little lanes. I say, any more of the local cider, courtesy of the Widow?' By Saturday's Bloody Mary time – 'Put fresh basil in it, trick I learnt from the barman when we were on a yacht in Turkey' – Charlie feels as if he's being treated as a waiter. Whizzy Fortescue, who put charming books and her best roses in the spare room, is mortified because Amanda complains about the pillows. 'I can only sleep on pure goosedown, Whizzy. And my friend at Villa San Michele could get linen sheets for you – there's a little shop by the Palazzo Pitti where they make them to measure for Ralph Lauren.' Whizzy, struggling with the eggy aftermath of breakfast (for Anthony and Amanda assume domestic fairies are going to load the dishwasher), has a vision of Mrs Reason, the apostle of Eazy-care, tackling a 300-thread count with her Rowenta. Amanda has to be taken antiqueing, 'Although I expect it'll be tat. The place to pick up marvellous things these days is Brussels – Rocco Forte has a sweet new hotel there.' While Whizzy is laying the table for 12 for dinner, Ant and Amanda have a siesta. 'We're exhausted – you're so lucky living in the country doing nothing all week.' On Sunday they let the newspapers blow all over the garden, demand constant fresh coffee, and Stinker, Ant's terrier, savages the Fortescues' rescue dog.

The Eligible Englishman

PEREGRINE, 18TH EARL of Posset, has seven Rembrandts, three Monets, a particularly gloomy Vermeer and a fossil collection once praised by Mark Girouard in *Country Life*. He is thus assumed to be fabulously rich. Ambitious mothers, with Arabellas and Sophies on the cusp of their fine-art degrees at Brown, are enchanted when Peregrine dismisses his Van Dycks as mere family portraits. What modesty in one so blessed, and how romantic dear Peregrine is, with his Cavalier ancestors and their sweet, ringletted children and charming King Charles spaniels. In fact, Peregrine has the disposition of an indigent weasel, the Rembrandts and the Monets are entailed, the fossil collection now diseased, and several of the Van Dycks are fakes.

Castle Posset's cover was blown when Cosima von Tulip arrived to stay with her own heater and demanded that the butler change the plug (Posset is still round-pin) so that she could dress for dinner without fear of frostbite. Peregrine doted on Cosima – so beautiful, so cultured, and with that little touch of the Wehrmacht, which he has always secretly admired. Cosima, having noted the wiring problem, the continuous brown food and Peregrine's cutaway chin, devastated him by saying that she really couldn't be Cosi Posset – it sounded like an Elizabethan herbal remedy. Until then, Peregrine had thought he was within touching distance of the Tulip fortune.

There was Sharon-Mae Schlumberger (the motor fortune), but her hair was really too blonde to go convincingly with tweed. There was Phoebe Sweeting, who embroidered velvet slippers with his heraldic crest, but sadly she came from Wilmslow. It would not do. She still sends him poems, and is the only woman who has never, ever remarked that his front teeth look like sawn-off stumps full of old compost.

Peregrine has the disposition of an indigent weasel

Naomi's smug assertiveness doing wheelies in haberdashery implies her divine right of motherhood

The Pushchair Terrorist

NAOMI HAS ALREADY ankle-capped a gentleman walking his labrador in St Leonard's Terrace, three elderly ladies in Waitrose and is now cutting a swath through Peter Jones. Couples doing their wedding list in china and glass are sundered by the ruthless progress of Naomi and Winkie; a Panzer division rarely achieved such destructive success. In the pushchair's wake seethe the halt and the lame. 'Bloody woman, why didn't she leave it at home with nanny?' And 'God, the fecund think they own the planet.' Those not rendered unconscious by having a steel vehicle rammed into their varicose veins wonder why a child capable of walking is being chauffeur-driven through soft furnishings.

Winkie is a lardy lump of fury who throws her teddy out of the pushchair when her mother is blocking the escalator. Kindly gay decorators, who've just come into PJs for 12 metres of silk dupion, rescue teddy from a horrible shredding in the escalator's teeth and are rewarded with a snatch and grab from Winkie's sticky fists. Naomi is sublimely ungracious. Her smug assertiveness doing wheelies in haberdashery implies her divine right of motherhood. Lifts empty at Naomi's approach, only the arthritic remaining pathetically pinned against the wall, whimpering as she reverses over their orthopaedic shoes. Strong women, who played hockey for their schools, are crippled as Naomi rams the pushchair towards the Clinique counter.

Winkie is now vociferous with boredom, heat and wants a drink of juice. 'Mummeee!' Naomi is oblivious to the surrounding volley of looks that could kill. Parenting classes have taught her that Winkie must be heard, and her verbalisation interpreted in a good way. Forcing the pushchair into a pinched Fulham hallway, releasing the tormented Winkie from chaffing safety straps, Naomi congratulates herself on her maternal dedication.

The Groundsman

ERNEST HAS BEEN the groundsman at Minster Lovage since the old king was alive. They tried to retire him in 1992, but he wouldn't trust anyone else with the roller. Tricky things, rollers, requiring an inordinate amount of oiling and tweaking. Not to mention the Atco. Locked up for its own protection – one never knows what the youth of today might get up to with a sit-on mower – the Atco dwells in the shed with the special measuring device for the white lines, a radio permanently tuned to Radio 2, a tool bench, kettle and a catering pack of PG Tips. What more could a man want?

It is a poignant time of year, for Ernest has just roped off his square against the predations of the footballers and rugby players. Should a ball land on the sacred sward, Ernest rockets from the shed, shouting, lest anyone breach the Maginot Line. Play has to be suspended while the offending object is retrieved with a rake. It was never like this when his lordship was at the manor, but a banker lives there now, and his children are football mad. A regrettable competitive edge has even crept into the village cricket matches of yore; Ernest thoroughly disapproves of the bankers' corporate bonding fixtures in which teams of accountants play estate agents, arriving in suspiciously clean Range Rovers with wives in high heels, a hideous threat to the field. They make Pimm's and fancy teas. Whither the egg sandwich, that's what Ernest would like to know. There was an unfortunate incident during the summer when a City type got knocked out cold by a cricket ball and the ambulance was summoned. For a terrible moment it seemed hell-bent on driving straight across the pitch, until Ernest flung himself in its path to direct it, agonisingly slowly, around the edge of the ground with windmill arm movements. Mortal injury is no excuse for showing a lack of respect to Ernest's wicket.

Ernest thoroughly disapproves of the bankers' corporate bonding fixtures

Claudette and the chipped fingernail have never been formally introduced

The Frenchwoman

THERE WAS THE magical moment when Chirac went wobbly on the war, and everyone thought Claudette would never be able to hold up her head in London society again. Not a bit of it. 'It is obvious ze Americans are war-mongering peegs,' she purred between little sips of champagne. 'This Bush needs to be beaten about.' It is one of Claudette's conceits that she thinks she has mastered idiomatic English. Almost as annoying as her perfectly matching ensembles, immaculate maquillage and divine manicure. Claudette and the chipped fingernail have never been formally introduced. It unnerves Englishwomen with cuticles toughened in the flowerbed. 'Bloody frogs, they're taking over everything in London: banks, our water companies, Claudette's husband is probably going to make the taps run with Evian. Do you know she takes the Eurostar to Paris just to have her hair done? Apparently no one here is good enough.' Actually, Claudette has been agreeably surprised by the English. She stayed in a charming cottage in Wiltshire with the Montmorencys. No matter that it was the Dower House, which Lady Montmorency was irked to have referred to as a cottage. English food has also proved tolerable, despite the frightful national habit of having jam with meat. Claudette's only concession to serious English food has been Mark's Club – 'Your bangers and mash eez so amusing.' At a dinner party in Holland Park, she nibbled a tiny mouthful and pronounced it 'Alors, really quite good' to a general exhalation of relief. The men, bemused by her foxy legs and aromatic cleavage wafting Chanel, get quite frisky. 'Your president looks like a drag queen, Claudette, and what have you got against the Americans? Coca-Cola?' Claudette is annoyingly robust with friendly fire that the euro is triumphing over the pound. She is also adamant that Concorde was French.

The Gentleman Cyclist

EDWARD HAS BEEN made to wear the skid-lid by his wife, Kitty, because she's convinced he is going to be crushed by a furious BMW driver and she and the twins will be left penniless in Battersea. Edward, stoically destroying his Welsh & Jefferies suit with a rucksack, bicycle clips and his luminous safety strap, says there's no need to get hysterical, he survived a Jeep rolling over his left leg while he was on a TA exercise. It was, however, a mistake to leave the *London Cyclist* quarterly in the hall, because Kitty read the article on the wrong sort of saddles causing sterility. There was no end of a fuss until he persuaded her that his trusty old Raleigh did not constitute a threat to their ongoing family life. 'Can't abandon the bike, old girl. It would take me forever to get to the office. Only last Tuesday I passed Bertie Fothergill walking to the Tube and, blow me down, I was at my desk, second cup of coffee in hand, before he even shimmered through the door.'

On wet days he attaches an umbrella to the handlebars, all the better to roll up and berate damned taxis with at the traffic lights. The cheek of some drivers. Edward believes in a conciliatory approach, but did not appreciate being called a sweaty tosspot by a cabbie with a tattoo reading I Love Doris up his forearm. Edward is particularly sensitive about sweat – as a stockbroker, one has to be; one has people to take out to lunch – and always cycles slowly, in high gear, since there are no showers at Proudlock and Punt. Sometimes he runs little errands for Kitty on the way home, like buying crystalised orange for the Christmas cake at Fortnum's. The bike's a blessing. Edward's only regret is that they don't make morning suits like they used to, with buttons to hook up the bottom of the tailcoat. On his way to a wedding the other day he had to use string and bulldog clips.

Edward did not appreciate being called a sweaty tosspot by a cabbie
with a tattoo reading I Love Doris up his forearm

Nil by mouth is Jessica's mantra; quite apart from making one fat, it might also necessitate more collagen injections around the mouth

The High-maintenance Woman

JESSICA HAS A serious problem. One of her eyelash extensions has fallen off. No matter that her eyeballs feel as if they are being scraped by broken glass every time she blinks: Jessica is now terrified that she looks as if she has mange. Really, life is so difficult. Bastien, the pedicurist at Claridge's, has a three-month waiting-list, her personal yoga trainer is away realigning Julia Roberts, and no one in London can wax eyebrows properly. She is mildly excited – an emotion difficult to express as her forehead's paralysed by Botox injections – by a new Wellbeing Treatment with personalised essential oils. But where to find the time? Drinking three litres of water a day is *so* onerous, there's hardly a moment to get to Space NK to buy the new Laura Mercier Secret Camouflage concealer.

Jessica never drives herself (the accelerator pedal is too damaging to Bastien's pedicure) nor cooks, since her fingernails might chip on a radicchio leaf. Gardening could precipitate a crisis with her back, which Barry at Claridge's has massaged ceaselessly (he's done wonders for Naomi Campbell). Her husband says that as she spends her entire bloody time at Claridge's, why doesn't she have several glasses of champagne and a jolly lunch in Gordon Ramsay's restaurant? Jessica goes quite white. Champagne is diuretic, and lunch is a time when Luke Hersheson in Conduit Street could be doing one's hair colour. Nil by mouth is Jessica's mantra; quite apart from making one fat, eating anything makes it more difficult to floss. Her best friend Rosie asks why Jessica's life is circumscribed by therapists when she is already so beautiful, but Jessica fails to see why she should take advice from a woman who has never suffered a bikini wax.

The English Dog at Home

BRANSTON AND PICKLE seized the high ground of the best chair during the port. It was while everyone was listening to Algy Baring's story about Bark, Offenbark and Depussy that the dogs made their excuses and left to disembowel a yard of Bendicks bittermints. By the time the dinner party comes through for The Game there is a trail of silver foil across the drawing-room. Lady Margot, wafting a Sobranie in an ebony holder, says isn't Branston a good chap? 'I've always hated Bendicks, vastly inferior to Good Boys in my view, so self-sacrificial of him to eat them,' she adds, plumping up a Colefax cushion for his head. Her guests arrange themselves carelessly on the floor and sagging chair arms while Algy energetically mimes Pope's *The Rape of the Lock*.

It is at this point that Pickle's bottom makes a smile, as Margot calls it. Robin clutches his throat and does the clothes-peg-on-nose routine – 'Margot, I can't think why you feed him that Fortnum's potted chicken, and his breath's a scorcher at the other end.' Margot bristles. 'Pickle's breath is pure eau de cologne,' and Pickle sticks his rogue tooth out with pleasure as his tummy is rubbed consolingly. His father, Chutney, became synonymous with fox poo after he rolled in it and rubbed himself against the treasurer's wife at the annual drinks party for the Conservatives. 'Your doggy is so affectionate, Lady Margot,' she'd said; but the butler heard her hiss on the way out, 'Horrid hairy little scrubbing brush, and as for Lady Margot's watered silk curtains, I can see what watered them.'

Some towny guests secretly think that Branston and Pickle should be called Keith and Prowse, 'because they always get the best seats in the house', but weekend habitués at Mere Manor are comforted by Pickle's presence when Margot says, 'Darling, it seems a bit chilly, shall we put another dog on your bed?'

Some towny guests secretly think that Branston and Pickle should be called Keith and Prowse, 'because they always get the best seats in the house'

We are going to the Maldives. I have booked. You only have to flop off the beach to see a teardrop butterfly-fish

The Winter Sunseekers

DERMOT AND VIRGINIA are embracing barefoot luxury. They have been delivered to their over-water villa in the Maldives by canoe, which Dermot thinks is pretty rum. Some chance of room service, eh? Damn ice will have melted by the time his G&T gets to him via the 'personal butler' on a pedalo. What was wrong with the Saint Geran in Mauritius? Marvellous place, terrific service, a chap in white shorts used to whizz up and clean his sunglasses on the beach. But Virginia is a winter sun snob. 'Everyone is talking about the Maldives this year, Dermot — water villas, the spas, the snorkelling. We are going to the Maldives. I have booked. You only have to flop off the beach to see a teardrop butterfly-fish.' So here they are, paying a fantastic amount of money to be marooned on their sundeck. Dermot wouldn't recognise a teardrop butterfly-fish if it sobbed on his shoulder, and is rather missing old Jeffrey Archer. 'Can't seem to find a good holiday read. When do you think they get the *Daily Telegraph* around here?' Irregularly, Virginia imagines, unless the message in a bottle system has yet to be perfected, and swims to the spa.

She's kept her figure through gardening and splendid genes, never allows the sun on her face — a shady brim is her style statement — and is going to be exfoliated with sea salt and sesame oil. Dermot wonders if she'll consequently be spitroast for the resort's beach barbecue welcome party. Sweating profusely, he's retreated to watch BBC World on a plasma screen in their air-conditioned thatched rondavel. Virginia writes a postcard to the poor Pritchards (farming being so dismal these days) saying it's marvellous how the sweet Maldivians seem to be able to grow organic vegetables. Once home, they'll entertain their bridge friends by saying how peacefully simple it all was. 'Imagine! Our butler delivered croissants by boat.'

The Archers Addict

JESSICA IS FROZEN with shock mid-dog-feeding. Siobhan has just let slip to Lizzie that Brian is the father of her baby. It can be only a matter of time now. Jennifer will find out, probably when Kate arrives from South Africa with Nolly, the child everyone says is so enchanting, but no one ever mentions is black. 'Sshh, Tregorran,' she says to her dog, who is attempting to remind her about his dinner. It is a particularly tense moment within the trusty Roberts radio as Lizzie tells Nigel she needs to ask Jill for advice. Jessica is absolutely with Nigel in categorically forbidding Lizzie to do any such thing. During the 20 years Jessica has been listening to *The Archers*, Jill's prime function has been to bake cakes, not to adjudicate on adultery. Her Victoria sponge might fail to rise, and then what would Bert have for his tea? As the radio trills tumpty-tum-te-tumpty-tum the dogs yelp with excitement, knowing starvation no longer stares them in the face.

When Jessica went to stay with Philippa in Languedoc, they had to tune Sky Television to Radio 4 so they could listen, crouched in the study with a bottle of rosé, staring at the screen as if Sid and Joleen were about to appear in living colour, line-dancing at the Bull. Moira, who's an intellectual, can now get episodes on her laptop on the BBC website, which has made travelling possible. Jessica's friend Ned says this is cheating, one should listen at home on a daily basis, with a dry martini, but he's a purist and won't even do the omnibus edition, although he admits Jessica has seized the moral high ground by having a neighbour who's a relation of the Earl of Portland, who acts David Archer. Jessica is not sure acting comes into it. One Saturday morning she woke, thrust open the windows and said, 'Thank the Lord, the sun's shining for Shula's wedding.'

As the radio trills tumpty-tum-te-tumpty-tum the dogs yelp with excitement, knowing starvation no longer stares them in the face

*He never replies to invitations; one never knows what might come up
– dinner with Vivien Duffield, a summons from Lady Black or a
glittering descent upon London by Carla Powell*

The Arrogant Guest

OSSIAN CONSIDERS YOUR party greatly blessed by his presence, which can only have come upon you as a delightful surprise, since he never replies to invitations. One never knows what else might come up – dinner with Vivien Duffield, a summons from Lady Black or a glittering descent upon London by Carla Powell (all too rare now she has this wretched new house near Rome). He only commits to the Royal Opera House after careful inquiry. Is the box on the left hand side, so as to be convenient for dinner in the Floral Hall during the interval? 'You're dining afterwards? My dear Claudia, even for you, and the joy of Mozart and the temptation of the excellent fishcakes at the Ivy, it would be too shatteringly late. You will have to forgive me.' The astonishing thing is that people do, even the hostesses who have never received a weekend present when they've invited him to stay. Should he come to such a lowly form of entertainment as drinks, he will say neither hello nor goodbye, just be a shimmering vision in Shanghai Tang, condescending only to talk to Emma Fellowes.

A little buzz of excited whispering reverberates in his wake: 'Ossian came! Tessa and Johnny must be thrilled.' Johnny and he were together at Winchester. 'Ossian? Funny old stick, never have discovered what he does. Shipping? MI6 perhaps – he went to Cambridge, of course.' It is Ossian's marvellous taste that has made his reputation, and a slight but waspish novel that had him hailed as the new Evelyn Waugh. It was so frightfully good he has never written another. The collection of Regency furniture in his set in Albany is fabled, and quite sensible women act upon his whims. 'We've dug up all the daffodils in the drive, Ossian says they're common.' As it's February, he's off to terrorise the matrons of Palm Beach for the winter season, the perpetual houseguest who never writes thank-you letters. It's too middle-class.

The married women don't want her in case she nicks their husbands

The Newly Divorced Woman

JULIA FEELS MARGINALISED, a pariah, damaged goods adrift at the great drinks party of life. Whenever two people are huddled together she imagines they are discussing how Kenneth informed her by e-mail from the first-class Silver Egret lounge at Singapore that he'd left with Charlene, the Australian help. They were on their way to 'finding themselves' in Bali. Since Kenneth had hitherto been incapable of finding so much as a sock without Julia's help, she sincerely doubts his capability to discover an inner self. So, at first, she was confident Kenneth would be back, and it could all be brushed over as an unfortunate incident. Julia has read about mid-life crises in her *Daily Mail*, and was prepared to be magnanimous, so she just told everyone in the Cobblers Heath bridge circle that he was away on business, and that now Imogen was at boarding school, they didn't need 'dear Charlene' any more.

Her mistake was confiding in Sylvia Pilcher over coffee and biscuits after their Pilates class. Sylvia, who detected her husband's affair with their nanny via animal groans on the baby alarm, could not resist telling Gill Sowerby. Then the news ripped through the tennis club's tournament in aid of the RNLI and the quiz night for St Augustine's church roof fund. Suddenly, Julia's world of solid coupleness, doing couple things, is rent by suspicion. The married women don't want her in case she nicks their husbands, and the single women regard her as unacceptable competition for men already earmarked. Thus Julia is mortified, but most particularly by the gin-flushed men who clap her on the shoulder, saying, 'Cheer up, old girl, you're still a fine figure of a woman, in with a chance. Most divorcees these days are either mad or have four children. By the way, Mitzi and I were thinking of going to Bali for our hols – love to look Ken up.'

31

They are confronted by Geoffrey Clifford fulminating in a bow tie

The Country Dinner Guests

HETTY AND GILES have disastrously misunderstood 'Woldshire casual'. They've only just moved to Piddle Wallop, and when Anne Clifford rang and asked them to dinner at the Old Manor – 'nothing smart, just us and the Greigs, they're about your age, so just Woldshire cas' – they were very touched. Now they are confronted by Geoffrey Clifford fulminating in a bow tie. An aged smoking jacket, silk lapels marinated in port stains, is clearly the only concession he feels a gentleman should make to 'casual'. Beyond, through a hall bristling with antlers, Giles sees Peregrine Greig in the accepted uniform, down to the velvet slippers embroidered with his crest. God, he was always an idiot at Eton. Hetty, in Boden, which is what she thought people wore in the country, doesn't need to be reassured by Anne Clifford – 'My dear, how lovely that you felt you knew us well enough not to dress up' – to know that she should have worn silk Moschino like Fenella Greig, who's now patronising her. 'We're all terrified of you, Hetty. I read the piece about your interior design company in *House & Garden* – are you going to do a Trinny and Susannah on all our houses?' Suddenly the welcoming fold of village life seems like a mare's nest.

'Such fun to hear news from Bohemian London,' says Anne Clifford over the vichysoisse. 'Geoffrey and I don't quite have straw for brains. We've been to see *The Lion King*.' Hetty realises country life is horribly inverted. Dizzy with the fatigue of working in London, she's come to the country to chill, not to be surrounded by people using smoking jackets and big jewellery as a defence mechanism against her Londonness. When she and Giles leave (having not yet learnt how dangerous it is to leave a country dinner first), the Cliffords and the Greigs reassure themselves with a good laugh about Hetty's 'designer trainers'.

The Merchant Banker

HOWARD IS ON his way to Frankfurt to meet Kurt, who is coming from Geneva to meet Hans, who has just been in Hong Kong meeting Hai Lo. It could all be done by conference call, but Morgan Gnome has a whites-of-their-eyes policy and Howard would feel completely disorientated if he was not in perpetual motion. Every morning he's up at five to check the Hang Seng Index while he is on his rowing machine, and the Nikkei while he's on the running machine. Then, after low-fat muesli, decaffeinated espresso and perfunctorily kissing his wife, he reads the *FT* in his chauffeur-driven car. The Morgan Gnome building was designed by Norman Foster, and Howard rides up in a glass elevator through an atrium filled with palm trees to his own vast, empty office on the top floor where his PA is waiting with chilled Evian. Howard takes his water very seriously. His last assistant was fired for providing the Evian in plastic, not glass bottles. Jeannine – a glossy, Armani-clad brunette – knows exactly how he likes everything. It is her primary concern, along with ensuring that he is never available. Howard would not be where he is today if he'd been available.

After lunch at the new, low-fat Savoy Grill, he works until late, then leaves for the airport, shouting at Chuck down his mobile in New York as he prowls through the club-class lounge.

'I'm coming in first-class BA on Tuesday, Chuck. We've got to kick this Conglomerated Biscuits deal into action. Where's the movement? ConBix can go global. I'm seeing Hans, who's seen Hai Lo. Hai says to say hi, by the way, I think he's with us.' Howard's children dimly remember him as the bloke in the penguin-motif bathing shorts (bought by Jeannine) when they were on holiday at Lyford Cay.

Howard would feel completely disorientated if he was not in perpetual motion

The Pushy Mother

HENRIETTA PLAYED MOZART to her bump during pregnancy because she'd read an article which said it would make the baby receptive to artistic impulses. And indeed, Toby could thump and dribble on the ivories virtually as soon as he was on solids. Henrietta instantly enrolled him on a Suzuki violin course. Her husband said he'd come home early of an evening in order to read *Winnie-the-Pooh* to the lad, and didn't expect him to be playing with zucchini. Henrietta said he wasn't to be ridiculous, but speak to Toby in German, because we are all part of the EU now, and Toby will be an über-banker just as soon as he's got his double first. Meanwhile, Portia needs her alphabet cards, and Henrietta really has to get to the PTA meeting because she promised Mrs Hogwash that she would hand round the crisps. Toby is currently doing the statutory project on Egypt, and Henrietta has reacted with the intensity of Lord Carnarvon, downloading cross-sections of the pyramids from the internet and taking him to see the mummies at the British Museum on Sunday.

As Toby comes up to common entrance, Henrietta will buy supplementary educational books at Smith's, based on his syllabus and with the answers in the back. 'We're getting up early each morning and working really hard,' she says brightly, having driven Toby to extra Latin in Fulham before breakfast. When he is having football coaching on Saturdays, Henrietta takes Portia to Tate Modern to improve her finger painting. While the children are at school, or swimming lessons, or supplementary kick boxing, Hen goes to the gym so that she doesn't let them down in the mothers' race. That she judges her happiness by her children's achievements may have a hideous nemesis: Toby's lifetime ambition will materialise as living in a bender in Wales.

*That she judges her happiness by her children's achievements may
have a hideous nemesis*

The Kept Man

CARLOS MET JULIA at Club 55 in St Tropez: she had descended from her villa in the hills and he was on the Popadopouloses' yacht. Carlos likes yachts, he looks very fetching flexing his chest hair on deck and Greeks can bear as many gifts as they like as far as he's concerned. He had been taking all the women around the St Trop market on Saturday morning, advising tirelessly on baskets, and then Julia, an old friend of Alexander Popadopoulos, joined them for lunch. He playfully scooped the crudités up, and under her straw hat (marvellous for shading her lines), she was entranced – 'So few men treat me as a woman, rather than a film star' – and he never got back on the boat again. Julia bought him an entire new wardrobe, he redesigned her pool cottage, and they became quite skittish listening to Bel Amour in the VIP section of Les Caves du Roy.

Then they returned to London, to her flat in Cadogan Square, and he's never quite made it home to Chile. He's always going next week, because of his business interests – much too complicated to explain – but then Jules needs him at a party in Mustique or a dinner with Nicky Haslam at the Ivy. 'Carlos, darling, you really can't go to Rio now, just be an angel and go and collect my prescription from the chemist, would you? And shall I wear the red or the blue dress?' Carlos, who has several sisters, is imbued with endless patience for waiting outside Valentino's changing rooms. And, having been brought up in the Andes, he is very good at carrying vast amounts of luggage at high altitude, which in Julia's experience means private jets. He is, she says as she slips him the money for lunch at San Lorenzo, the first man who has been really there for her.

Julia's only fear is that Carlos will run off with an older woman.

Carlos likes yachts, he looks very fetching flexing his chest hair on deck

Sylvia then puts on a CD of whale music and makes mint tea in little pink Moroccan glasses

The Lifestyle Guru

SYLVIA OPENS WIDE her arms to let in the energy. 'Reflect, rejoice, life is good. You have all the potential in the world.' She then sinks gracefully into the lotus position, and Joanna scrambles down after her like a camel. She is less than convinced by this lifestyle thingy and would prefer to be walking the dog. Sylvia says, spookily, 'I know you have inner doubts, Joanna, that it is difficult for you to let your mind float, but you will be calmer if you discover your inner karma.' Joanna's mind has actually been floating – towards Sainsbury's and the weekend shop and whether she will be able to get to Lucy's lacrosse match. 'Joanna, you must let go. I am here to restore you to yourself. You must make the time to be good to the inner you. You have a beautiful soul.'

Joanna is now feeling distinctly uncomfortable, not entirely the result of cranking herself into the lotus position. Is this woman going to force her into the shower and detoxify her with rock crystals? 'Joanna, I want you to feel more focused, more energised. I was once fat, and felt hopeless. Now I feel free to express my personality. Let us choose the light over the dark.' She then puts on a CD of whale music and makes mint tea in little pink Moroccan glasses. 'I think you are a pink person – we need to liberate the colour within you.' Joanna thinks of the five trusty black suits she wears to work, and the surprise with which she would be greeted at the office in a pink kaftan. 'I say, Sylvia, what I really wanted to talk to you about was time management, which doesn't include drinking mint tea.' Sylvia smiles her maddeningly serene smile. 'But it should, Joanna. You are depriving yourself. And may I just say – just a small suggestion, but the small things are so vital in our lives – that one's hair colour really mustn't drain from the natural skin tone.' Joanna is livid. Who is a woman who lives with cats in Islington to lecture her on highlights?

41

The Christmas Guest

DEAN IS AMERICAN and fastidious. He likes neither children nor dogs, which, with unerring sensitivity, have pinioned him on the sofa. The dog is drooling over his Polo Ralph Lauren chinos with loving dribble; Lily and Pixie are asking what wishes he put up the chimney for Father Christmas, and did he really buy his Christmas presents for them in New York, as Mummy said, and was America full of fat people, like Daddy said, and did he have a fridge full of ice-cream, as Granny said all Americans did, and had he brought it with him?

Dean, a fragile merchant banker (if such a thing were possible), is having a panic attack. It had seemed such a nice idea, spending Christmas at the Old Rectory with the Lindsays. Charlotte Lindsay is a lovely person, warm and welcoming, and Hugo was one of the few people he met in the banking fraternity who didn't overtly patronise him for being Dean Pozanski Jr. 'I say, Dean, if you're not going home to New York, Charlotte would love you to come to us at Christmas. It's a family thing: the gargoyle of a mother-in-law, screaming children, dodgy heating – we'd love to have you, if you can put up with us.' And Charlotte rang to say how thrilled they'd be, and the guest bedroom was really quite comfortable, although the basin gurgled a bit. And would he mind awfully sharing a lav with the Croatian au pair? Charmed by this artlessness, Dean is entirely unprepared for childish excitement, alcoholic excess, Charlotte being reduced to tears by burnt mince pies or being the buffer zone between Hugo and the mother-in-law. Yet his presents are a wow – particularly the pashmina for the gargoyle, and Rapunzel Barbie for Lily – and afterwards everyone (particularly Mrs Pilsley, the housekeeper to whom he's slipped £50) says, 'It was really nice having Dean. Can he come again next year?'

Dean is entirely unprepared for childish excitement, alcoholic excess or his hostess being reduced to tears by burnt mince pies

*Nothing in Sabrina's experience of doing the PR for Shimmer
Lipsticks had prepared her to be a nanny*

The Father's Girlfriend

SABRINA WANTS ADRIAN'S children to like her, she really does. Though a stranger to the domestic arts, she has slaved long and hard over a salad and is now hoping for happy little faces. 'I hate tomatoes,' says Jeremy. 'Mummy never uses tuna because dolphins get trapped in the fishing nets and die,' says Chloe. Phoebe bursts into tears. It is at this point that Adrian walks in, peers into the offending salad bowl and says, 'Darling, that looks marvellous, what a bore I can't eat anchovies.' Jeremy smirks. Sabrina bursts into tears; it wasn't meant to be like this, she didn't break up his beastly marriage. When she met Adrian at the Cliffords' he was so funny and handsome, yet vulnerable. His estranged wife was obviously terribly tough, obsessed with her career. Sabrina thought she could heal his pain. In her mind's eye this meant dinners at Le Caprice and a villa in Tuscany, not a cottage in Cornwall with three gargoyles who chorused 'Are we there yet?' all the way from Heston services. Chloe said that if she didn't sit in front with Daddy she'd be sick. It has rained every day. At midnight, just when Sabrina thought she was safely alone with her beloved, Phoebe burst into the bedroom howling that she had a pain in her tummy.

Nothing in Sabrina's experience of doing the PR for Shimmer Lipsticks had prepared her to be a nanny. Since Chloe tried on all her shoes and used her make-up to turn Phoebe into a Pirate Princess, Sabrina feels as if the wicked stepmother genie has stolen her privacy. Also, her clothes that would have been so enticingly romantic in San Gimignano are curiously inappropriate for Padstow. Now she's been labelled a dolphin-hating witch. Could she stand having Chloe and Phoebe as bridesmaids? Strangely, when Sabrina is replaced by Angie next summer, the children will say, 'Sabrina was ace. She made us grown-up food and had cool clothes.'

The Coffee Bar Scene

NINA HAS BEEN to Covent Garden flower market, dropped off
her son for extra Latin coaching and is on her way to the gym, a
routine punctuated by a skinny latte decaf macchiato. Edward is
taking Poppy to school, giving her a honey and raisin bran muffin
by way of breakfast, her mother still being in bed, exhausted by
their month in the south of France. 'Nina! Lovely to see you. How
was your summer?' Really, Starbucks is too social these days. It's
horribly early for Edward's charm to be frothing all over her, like
his cappuccino. Poppy is whining: 'Come on, Papa. Miss Benham
will be weally cwoss if I'm late.' Edward shimmers out the door.
'Bye, must get this little horror to prison. Now we're all back from
the hols you have to come round to dinner.' The student reading
Kafka rolls her eyes at this bourgeois badinage.

Nina sinks back into her *Daily Mail* until Arabella arrives, drag-
ging her dachshund along the pavement and peering into the fog
of almond croissants. 'Nina? God, I haven't got my lenses in. Let me
just tie Widget to a chair outside. I'll die if I don't have a caffeine
fix.' This takes an inordinate amount of time as Arabella gets stuck
behind a man with no conception of Starbucks etiquette, saying,
'What do you mean, with froth or without? I just want a normal
cup of coffee. At £2.25 it shouldn't be bloody impossible.' With
sinking heart Nina recognises the obdurate tones of a Hampshire
neighbour. 'Nina? God, what a nightmare. Can't get a decent cup
of Nescafé for love or money. Had to come up last night, got an
early meeting at Sotheby's.' Widget has wound himself round a table
leg, yelping as Arabella spills her grande skinny cappuccino-to-go
on his tail. The Kafka student has been joined by a beard clutching
Thomas Mann, and looks quite pink. It's time for Nina to go to the
anonymity of the gym.

It's horribly early for Edward's charm to be frothing all over Nina,
like his cappuccino

The Treatment Addict

GINA'S AMBITION TO unblock her energy channels by having hot stones placed on her chakra points is mildly impeded by her inability to switch off the mobile. The office needs her, despite the difficulty of discussing market strategy while balancing a pebble on her forehead. There was once an unfortunate incident when the patchouli oil being poured on to Gina's third eye dribbled on to her Nokia, and she sprang out of the Krishna Centre for Beauty Synergy with half her dead cells unexfoliated.

Now, lying in a fug of jasmine candles, she is trying to book a silver ion facial for when she arrives in LA. No matter that she will have to wear a leather mask disturbingly similar to Hannibal Lecter's, positive and negative charges will simultaneously infuse minerals and expel toxins from her skin. A real silver galvanic compound will enhance Gina's absorption of vitamins, an effect that will, in all likelihood, be diminished by her intake of Marlboro Lights. God, the stress of having to choose between microdermabrasion and a paraffin pedicure. And what is it all for? In her darker moments (when she is sporting a chilled lavender eye-mask) Gina reflects that the silver galvanic compound hasn't had the electrifying effect seen on Sophie Dahl. So far Keanu Reeves has not yet been galvanised into beating a path to her Battersea door. It is at these difficult moments that the grim spectre looms of going to the gym, or – worse – on a diet. Then Gina reads about intense pulsed light therapy – the photo facial – in American *Vogue*. One paparazzi-like flash of IPL, her body's reparative mechanisms will be stimulated and Gina's outer Vanessa Feltz will be replaced by her inner Gwyneth Paltrow.

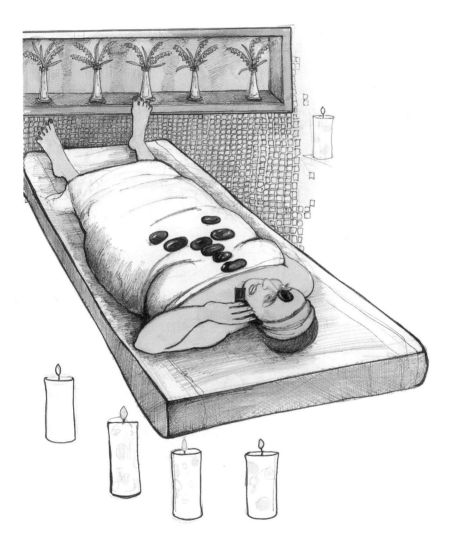

There was once an unfortunate incident when the patchouli oil being poured on Gina's third eye dribbled on to her Nokia

The Father at the Teenage Ball

HENRY IS LIVID. He hasn't been able to have a drink all evening because of picking up these wretched children from Hammersmith Palais. Sarah said she wasn't going to do it, not having cooked them a dinner party, frisked them for alcohol and worried herself sick about Poppy Morrison's story of almost having a syringe injected into her bottom in the loo at the Plume Ball last year. Henry says it's all a lot of damned nonsense. Now he's a desperate man. All the children streaming out of the dance look eerily alike. What was the point of Perdita saying, 'Daddy, you'll recognise me by the pink pashmina'? All the girls have pink pashminas and curtains of blonde hair. Torquil was expedited looking immaculate in a perfect dinner jacket bought for £15 from Oxfam, which bears no relation to the boys emerging with their bowties ripped off and shirt tails hanging out. And the idiot has turned off his mobile. All the girls are barefoot and limping because it is the first time they have worn high heels.

Sarah, crouched over a second bottle of Pinot Grigio is now hysterical. 'Henry? You'll have to go in. Torquil may be drowning in his own vomit.' Henry would rather go over the top at the Somme. 'I might miss him, old girl, calm down now. Don't panic, Captain Mainwaring! Remember he said that all he wanted to do was get sweaty and snog a lot of girls?' Perdita finally emerges in tears because her pashmina has a cigarette burn, and someone's groped her emergency £10 note out of her bra; Torquil lopes out with his DJ rolled up in a plastic bag sticky with beer. 'It was cool, Dad. Where were you? All these Range Rovers look alike. Grunter Howard's coming to spend the night. Can you make sure Mum doesn't wear an embarrassing nightie?'

Henry's a desperate man: all the children streaming out of the dance look eerily alike

Libby's Sharp Intake of Breath is a performance of exquisite hyperventilation presaging a width restriction

The Back-seat Driver

LIBBY PUMPS HER foot on an imaginary brake and shrills, 'Have you seen that pedestrian? Have you, Brian?' while in the dim distance a lone figure is inching towards the Belisha beacon on a Zimmer frame. 'Not exactly the type to spring impulsively into the traffic, I think,' says Brian, his knuckles whitening through the holes in his leatherette driving gloves. But Libby is giving her Sharp Intake of Breath, a performance of exquisite hyperventilation presaging an imminent width restriction. 'Careful, Brian, careful. Judge your width. You've two inches on this side, hold her steady now.' Brian feels as if the Mondeo has become a battleship negotiating the Panama canal. Libby is now flourishing the map, which involves much paper-crackling to get the creases in the right place for the journey to the Peak District, as well as a magnifying glass. Libby is minutely prepared for all motoring eventualities, including snow in June, since she has checked the de-icer in the boot and the windscreen scraper. 'Only 20 years ago snow stopped the cricket at Buxton. I think we have to err on the safe side. Now, Brian, it's the second left off the roundabout. Mind that lorry.'

Brian test-drove one of those cars with a Margaret Thatcher living in the dashboard, giving directions in synthesised elocution: 'Turn right here for the A123, and proceed in an easterly direction.' He thought it would save Libby map-reading and give him and Classic FM some peace, but Libby disagreed with Maggie and said that no one with any sense would use the A123 – particularly as there were roadworks at the junction with the B456 – and as a result she over-rode the instructions for the entire journey, and a 20-minute excursion to Reading took an hour and a half, with Libby shouting furiously at the dashboard. After this fracas, the Sharp Intake of Breath comes as a mild blessing.

The New Year's Eve Haters

JULIAN AND EDWINA are hibernating with the cat. Julian would rather have cyanide poured down his ear than go to a New Year's Eve party. Edwina says New Year's Eve is common, has turned up the heating and is reading Selina Hastings's biography of Rosamond Lehmann. Julian and the cat, Ozymandias, are huddled over Andrew Barrow's *Quentin and Philip*. He'd thought of editing some page proofs but the standard of authors at Rutledge Keegan Charter Headstart is now so dismal that he could not add to the depression of New Year's Eve by tackling their dank oeuvres. What was wrong with the old year, that's what he'd like to know. Just as he got used to it, the damn thing is making for the exit.

Edwina, who errs on the side of global gloom, foresees the Third World War with Mr Bush's on-going plans. She has dire forebodings about the Tube: 'Julian, you are absolutely not to go on the Undie, think smallpox carriers.' Julian says at least they won't take up as much room as the people carrying backpacks.

He then puts on his Bose headphones (a Christmas present) to listen to *Siegfried* at full throttle, but without betraying to the neighbours that they are in. Edwina and Julian are under self-imposed house arrest; in the flat below, Sam and Jodie are giving a party – 'Hey, it'll be really fun, you guys gotta come' – and Edwina said how perfectly lovely, but they were away. Hence the curtains are drawn, the lights low, Edwina barefoot so as not to make a noise trotting to the kitchen for some fresh foie gras. Utter horror as she inadvertently knocks over the bottle of wine. Will Sam and Jodie hear? Worse, ring the police suspecting burglars? Julian, wrenching Wagner off his ears, says he thinks it highly unlikely anyone is going to apprehend a bottle of his best Leoville Barton crashing to the floor through the vulgar cacophony of Auld Lang Syne.

Julian is listening to Siegfried at full throttle: Edwina says
New Year's Eve is common

*Jane cannot enter Polly's bedroom without crunching jewellery,
hair products and CD cases underfoot*

The Teenager's Mother

NEVER, EVER DID Jane imagine that a child could have the power to reduce her to a jibbering, stressed-out harridan. She's always addressing her daughter's back as Polly saunters out the door, impervious to Jane's inquisition about why the computer is still on. 'And when did the floor become a wardrobe-substitute?'

Jane cannot enter Polly's bedroom without crunching jewellery, hair products and CD cases underfoot. The desk has disappeared under a pile of Topshop fake fur and denim, so Polly's geography project is now being done on the kitchen table. There's the continuing drama with the mobile phone which Polly is forever leaving down the back of the seat on the school coach. 'Polly?' Polly's eyes fail to disengage from *EastEnders*. 'Polly, we have found your mobile. I have rung Vodaphone and, using six passwords, undone the cancellation which I made yesterday on the 24-hour hotline. The coach driver is my new best friend. Polly? I'm too old to make new friends. You must take responsibility for your actions.' Polly says, 'OK, cool.'

Jane stomps out to cook supper. 'Oh Mum, meat, how gross. Didn't I tell you I'd become a vegetarian?' Jane says no, actually, she hadn't, since communication didn't seem to be her strong point, and when her father had asked her about the Feathers Ball – for which she, Jane, had taken so much trouble getting tickets – all Polly had mumbled was 'Good'. 'The only time you have been in any way loquacious this holidays is when you got on the wrong train to see Lucy, and left your laptop at the station. Who had to sort that out? Your mother. Me. I am not a chauffeur, or a lost-and-found service. Incidentally, that white thing below the microwave is the dishwasher. If you must eat cereal at midnight, please put your bowl into it.' Sobbing to *her* mother, Jane says she wouldn't mind, but why is it that 15-year-olds never smile?

Flora is motionless, arms clamped to her sides in case her deodorant has failed her

The Worrier

FLORA IS PANICKED that she might have spinach on her teeth. Or maybe her breath smells. She did clean her teeth obsessively before coming to the party, but one sip of champagne might have soured her efforts. She doesn't dare speak in case the oral equivalent of a flame-thrower, overlaid with Sensodyne Total Care, issues forth and catches Toby Pettifer amidships. Flora has always rather fancied Toby, who is now talking across her mute beauty to Jonty Bunting. The party is awfully hot, so as well as being wordless, Flora is also motionless, arms clamped to her sides in case her deodorant has failed her. And did she leave the iron on? She certainly put it upright, but did she turn it off at the wall? The telephone rang, it was Mummy, and maybe she forgot to unplug the iron because, as Mummy was telling her that the Chipchases were coming to lunch on Sunday, Flora remembered that she'd left the bath running. It was only last year that she was soaking her whites, got distracted by *EastEnders*, the bath overflowed and the ceiling of the downstairs flat collapsed. Daddy said she was a silly little muffin.

Now Toby is offering her a quail's egg, and she is so overcome she swallows it whole, and has to be hit on the back so it shoots out into Sophia Anstruther's sea breeze. Plop. Desperate mopping of Sophia's lavender silk camisole. 'I say, let me help,' says Toby enthusiastically, dabbing at Sophia's bosom with a red spotty hanky. Flora's kitten heel has caught in the seagrass carpet, so that she is welded to the spot as Toby leers at Sophia and Sophia says she is perfectly all right, really, lavender is so last year, and gosh, Toby, she'd love to go out to dinner. Flora finally utters, 'I must go, I've left the iron on.' And totters into the night on one shoe, a modern Cinderella.

59

The Amateur Dramatics Society

PAMELA IS THE leading light of the Chalfont St Oswald amateur dramatics society and always gives herself the most glamorous parts, preferably in fishnets to show off her legs, which Mrs Trubshawe the postmistress thought most unsuitable for the Fairy Godmother in *Cinderella* last Christmas. There was the time she cast her husband, Miles, as the giant in *Jack and the Beanstalk*, although he's a widdling 5ft 6in and highly nervous. Percy the publican, a 17st pachyderm who had been confident of getting the role, then refused to serve 'meek and Miles'.

This year the St Oswald's Players are staging *Little Red Riding Hood* – directed by Pam, with costumes designed by Pam, and written by Pam – with the wolf in a Tony Blair mask attempting to ban hunting so that he can be the only predator in the countryside. Pamela's diverted from the Brothers Grimm by writing herself a set-piece as Foxy, the lady who loves a chase, in a shameless cabaret sequence with all the members of the hunt high-kicking behind her.

At the dress rehearsal Kirsty, the doctor's receptionist who is playing Red Riding Hood, is furious that her forest-green dress, made on Mrs Trubshawe's old Singer, makes her look like a frilly Cox's Orange Pippin. It is these moments Pamela's son-in-law, coerced into service as the piano accompanist, annually dreads, and has to put his hands over his ears. On the night, in front of an audience fuelled by mulled wine, Brian the builder's MDF trees fall over, prompting cheery audience participation: 'Just like your houses, mate.' It's a tremendous success. Everyone says Pam's a marvel; what energy – where would the village be without her?

Pam's written herself a set-piece as Foxy, the lady who loves a chase

Many a thirtysomething has continued her gym membership just for the pleasure of seeing Oscar work on his abs

The Beautiful Boy at the Gym

OSCAR IS WRITING a film script. That is why he spends all his time at the gym, to avoid putting pen to paper. There was a cunning hiatus when his computer crashed, so he went to the gym even more to vent his artistic frustration. At least, that's what he told one of the yummy mummies who plied him with cappuccinos. 'Poor Oscar, did you lose everything?' she inquired, ogling his biceps as he lifted the frothing cup to his Cupid's bow lips. Oscar pouted, and said, 'Yeah, like it was just going so well. Spielberg's really, really interested.' In fact, Oscar hasn't got much further than fantasising about escorting Cameron Diaz up the red carpet at the Oscars. 'An Oscar for Oscar' – he can visualise the headlines as he works on his abs. Many a thirtysomething Susie or Camilla has continued her gym membership well beyond the obligatory new year puritanism just for the pleasure of seeing Oscar work on his abs. 'What's your script about, Oscar?' they ask girlishly, having spent hours before the school run achieving the glowing no-make-up look, so Oscar might walk them to their 4x4 in the car-park. 'Can I be a character in your movie, Oscar?' 'Well, Camilla, it's a wicked story – maybe we should talk about it.'

He tells Susie he comes to the gym for thinking time. Susie puts lip gloss on in the car mirror before arriving, and buys Oscar lunch. Still mineral water and bean sprouts at the health bar. 'Your life must be so glamorous,' she says, and Oscar shrugs, 'Yeah, well . . .' God, he's cool. And he lives in Notting Hill. 'Yeah, my dad's in the theatre.' What Susie and Camilla don't know is that Oscar's dad is a barman at the Gielgud, Oscar's real name is Darren, and he works shifts at Kwik-Fit Exhaust. It's a better story than the one he'll never write.

Bryony's spirit must fly, unfettered in the cosmos of creativity

The Child Prodigy

BRYONY COULD PICK out *Für Elise* on the piano at 18 months. Plonk, plonk, tinkle, plonk. Her father Gilbert has never ceased to tell Oxford dinner parties that this pre-dates evidence of the early infant genius of Mozart. Mozart was a dismally late developer at the age of three, by which time Bryony was sawing away at the violin and had written – well, trilled to Gilbert, because she couldn't write her own name, let alone musical notes – a symphony based on *The BFG*. The thunderous bass notes at the entrance of the giant indicate, Gilbert says, the profound effect of fairy tale on a sensitive artistic psyche. Bryony is quivering with sensitivity, unlikely as this may seem from the sad little pudding face.

Her mother, a fey vegetarian presence in hippie skirts, said Byrony really ought to go to school and make friends. But Gilbert was adamant. The rough and tumble of the playground might threaten Bryony's hands. Imagine if her index finger were thwacked by a flying Barbie. She might never play the violin again, and besides, Jessica Palmer, a history don's daughter, was shamelessly bullied in botany class. This sort of trauma is not for Bryony, her spirit must fly, unfettered in the cosmos of creativity. Hence Gilbert has taught Bryony himself, his efforts augmented by a succession of classics tutors and mathematics postgraduates. Bryony is alarmingly good at mathematics. She lisps French fluently now, and has a grasp of economics which would confound Gordon Brown. Her knowledge of current affairs is culled from the *Independent*, and the fact that she is allowed to watch only documentaries on television. Thus she has nothing in common with her peer group, who are obsessed with *24* and Topshop. By the time Bryony has won Musician of the Year she will be yearning to wear black lipstick and work as a waitress in Pucci Pizza.

The Blonde 4x4 Driver

ANDREA IS COMPLETELY oblivious to the universal expressions of contempt and loathing that follow her progress down the King's Road, since she is doing her make-up, checking her ash highlights in the rear-view mirror and having a frightfully urgent conversation on the mobile. 'Melissa, he's married; married men do not take one to Le Caprice, far too many people might see you. Married men take you to Paris. Don't stand for anything less. Oh, get out of the way, you silly old fool!' A Chelsea pensioner totters backwards from underneath Andrea's wheels. Zebra crossings mean nothing to her – animal prints are so last year – and small children in perambulators, confidently pushed out into the road by trusting Australian nannies, are a particular irritant. Being rather short, Andrea, craning over the dashboard, only dimly perceives small lives being snatched from under her bullbars – an essential for negotiating the speed bumps in St Leonard's Terrace.

A hooting, cursing queue builds up nicely behind her when she stops to retrieve a dropped mascara bottle from the deep litter of parking tickets on the floor. Frightful little wardens – don't they know about picking up fresh tuna from Harvey Nichols Fifth Floor? She was only on the double yellow line a minute. All the shiny Sloane Street shopping bags hurtle forward as she hits the brakes. 'Melissa, are you still there? God, these lights. Bloody Ken Livingstone, doesn't he realise that he's grinding this city to a halt? Melissa? Darling, don't give him presents, particularly not ties, he'll never be able to wear them. That his wife is a woad-wearing simpleton is exactly why she'd spot a swanky tie. Must go, I've found a Res Park.' Andrea manouevres by bumping the cars fore and aft out of the way, and wafts into Real Hairdressing on Chelsea Green to fulfil her blonde ambition. One can always be an icier shade of pale.

Zebra crossings mean nothing to her – animal prints are so last year

George now has a Beckham and says, 'Duh, Mum' when asked where those nice Gap chinos are

The Public Schoolboy

IT DRIVES GEORGE'S mother insane that the result of spending £17,000 a year on school fees has been to turn her son into Ali G. George's soul was supposed to be soaring to Keats, but he's come home with *FHM* magazine. The adorable, floppy-haired Hugh Grant that went off in its uniform, fresh-faced, now has a Beckham and says, 'Duh, Mum' when asked where those nice Gap chinos are. All George's sludge-chic clothing bears the nametapes of others. His mother, picking them up off his bedroom floor, wearily assumes there must be a circulating library of tracksuit bottoms. Somewhere, another mother is picking up the ones labelled GEJ Hamilton in Cash's green. And why didn't he tell her that he'd grown out of his school shoes? George grunts. His conversation, extracted in monosyllables by his parents ('How is your coursework on the Crusades, darling?'), consists of a half-swallowed mumble. The linguistic clouds only part when George lifts his head from biting his nails and says clearly, 'I have to have a laptop.' This joins other Have to Haves including Oakley sunglasses and Nike trainers. George's father says he'll be damned lucky, given his report, and could he please take his tin of Coke off the dining-room table and use a glass?

George ambles off to hang out in the King's Road, walking the public-school pimp-roll, dismissing his gross family with a languid arm covered in friendship bracelets from his hol in Cornwall. His sister screams after him, 'You've left the bathmat wet, and your room smells of armpits.' Oh, and he's lost his mobile. Duh. It is the only object with which he makes eye contact. Yet when he stayed with the Fretwells, Lucy rang afterwards and said, 'George was a dream, always offering to help, loading the dishwasher and sweet with the little ones.' George's mother said, 'Who is this person? I don't know him.'

The Pedicure Addict

LARA HAS DISCOVERED her feet. The epiphany happened in New York when a friend, shaken to the core by the sight of Lara's prehensile extremities in sandals – Park Avenue princesses don't do unvarnished toes – whisked her to the BuffSpa at Bergdorf Goodman. Clive plunged her yellowing soles into a postmodernist footbath full of pebbles. Clive massaged and exfoliated. Clive did not shrink from toenails like pork scratchings. Lara attained a catatonic state of ecstasy. Who needs a boyfriend? Sex? Please. Get Lara a foot god to shape her nails with a diamond file.

Back in London, Lara has become Foot Maintenance Woman, ever in pursuit of new feats of extravagance. There's Zeny, who does the weekly assault course on Lara's build-up in the lunch-hour at BestFeetForward. Zeny scrapes off hardened callus as brittle as parmesan shavings. There's Pilates foot exercise with the private instructor to straighten out her hammer toe: 'Now Lara, I'm going to spread these little silver balls on the floor and you're going to play Picking Up Cherries Under the Tree. Flex that toe, curl it round.' It seems a bit much at 6am, but Jimmy Choo, here comes Lara, walking on air, having spent the night in Bliss Spa gel socks.

After a revarnish she wears flip-flops in the snow, lest a smear should adulterate the perfection of her Thrash Metal polish. Her brother, with all the tact of an Old Etonian, asked whether she'd had a terrible accident, inadvertently crushing her toenails in a door. Lara retorted did he know he had hair growing out of his ears? She's been told about a marvellous women who plucks eyebrows – maybe she could help. For Lara's birthday party she has a girlie evening: champagne, M&S risotto, parma ham and figs (but no shaved parmesan), with Zeny to give pedicures. And the Pilates teacher. He's a dish.

70

Lara has become Foot Maintenance Woman, ever in pursuit of new feats of extravagance

There is a velvet-edged competitiveness about these lunches

The Girls' Lunch

CHARLOTTE, MIMI AND Tania are having lunch together so that they can talk about how awful men are. Tania's hoop earrings bounce with indignation as she discloses Rupert's transgressions. He likes Arnold Schwarzenegger films and rugby. Charlotte and Mimi flick their hair in sympathy, and Mimi says sweetly that she feels so lucky Cosmo only likes tennis and is a member of Queen's. 'The Stella Artois is so much more civilised than Wimbledon, and we always lunch with Frank Lowe. He invented the tournament, you know. Last year I sat next to Nigel Havers.'

There is a velvet-edged competitiveness about these lunches. When Tania goes to the loo, Charlotte will say to Mimi that Rupert is clearly an uncouth crasher who indubitably sweats in bed. Mimi murmurs demurely into her Pinot Grigio. In her little blonde innocent way she has told her saddo girlfriends that she has a cool boyfriend and hangs out with famous people. Charlotte is divorced ('But we're still each other's best friends'), and slightly older – enough to be agonised about whether to cut that waterfall of hair; the blowdrying is torture but it does keep her from having wobbly underarms. Charlotte keeps her powder dry until last. She has been made a director of her company; she is going to have to commute to New York – 'Such a bore. One will have to have replica Armani wardrobes' – but it will be fun to see more of Jake in the NY office because last week they had a really great evening at *The Producers*. 'He got Cameron Mackintosh's house seats.' Game, set and match. Charlotte has registered that she is a successful businesswoman with a designer wardrobe, a New York apartment and a serious man who can get impossible theatre tickets. And at least she's been married. Tania and Mimi suddenly feel very not grown-up. Outside Le Caprice, they all mwah-mwah and say they must have lunch again soonest, darling.

The Divorce Lawyer

EVERYONE TOLD MARIETTA that she should go to Fiona Blaby. 'She's a Rottweiler, she'll smash Julian into the ground, take him to the cleaners. You've got to do it, Marietta, after the way he's treated you.' Marietta is not at all sure she's got to do anything. She just wishes everything was all right again, and like it used to be, and the dog is so upset. Fiona Blaby has seen it all before. Bemused women walk into her office wanting an amicable divorce and walk out with their spines stiffened, determined that he's not going to get away with so much as the Peter Jones saucepans from their wedding list. Fiona is mustard on dog allowances: 'Come on, Marietta. Think of Petplan. I'm sure you want Bertie to be on the supreme insurance scale in case of vet's bills. This can cost £700 per annum, increasing with his age.' Marietta is appalled. It is the least Bertie deserves: only this morning, when she'd steamed open Julian's credit card statement, he loyally bounced up and down on the envelope with muddy paws, so she'd be able to say, 'The dog did it' when Julian questioned the scrumpled state of his mail. Fiona even makes inquiries about the guinea-pig. 'There is a woman in Los Angeles, Marietta, who gets a $1,500 monthly allowance for her child's rabbit.'

This attention to the minutiae of marriage has made Fiona more aggressively successful than her male colleagues, to whom guinea-pigs are little rats with sawn-off bottoms, not exquisite twists of the alimony knife. Her discreet, calm but terrible personal questions about conjugal relations and physical violence elicit descriptions of domestic scenes one would hardly have thought possible in a nice house in Wandsworth. As she sends Marietta off to itemise her jewellery and produce a year's Coutts bank statements, Fiona taps a blood-red nail on her partner's desk and reckons she's got Julian on toast.

Fiona asks discreet, calm but terrible personal questions about conjugal relations and physical violence

*So far Tweetie has nibbled one sugared almond in the shape of a
swaddled baby; she's just been so busy opening pressies*

The Baby Shower

TWEETIE'S BABY SHOWER is being given by Kimberley La Zouche, an absolute best friend. Tweetie's known her at least six months; they met at the New York collections when Tweetie was the catwalk sensation wearing Rogue's denim wedding dress trimmed with white marabou. It had been front-page news that very morning that she was expecting Jangles Mortimer's baby: 'Drummer and Supermodel to Wed'. Kimberley always has a front seat at the Rogue shows, and Rogue brought her backstage ('Tweets, this darling person can't wait to meet you'). And now here they all are, in Kimberley's penthouse in Eaton Square, drinking margaritas out of baby bottles. So far Tweetie has received an Hermès cashmere cot blanket, a Tiffany rattle and a blow-up baby bath in the shape of a yellow duck, with the technology to tell her (or nanny, more like) whether the water is too hot or too cold. She invited Kate and Claudia, and the air is heady with oestrogen and Rob Van Helden's flowers. Kimberley got ADC to do the catering, hot from parties for Mario Testino and Jade Jagger. They've recreated Asia de Cuba in the Zen roof garden and a champagne bar in the Jacuzzi.

So far Tweetie has nibbled one sugared almond in the shape of a swaddled baby; she's just been so busy opening pressies. The editor of *Vogue* brought a leather nappy bag from Semmalina, wrapped in silver cellophane and sequins. Her old schoolfriend Martha brought a teddy she'd wrapped herself; Kimberley was so shocked she shut it away in the cupboard. Tweetie is grateful to Kimberley – she'd been told that if no one offered you a baby shower, you weren't popular – and Jangles will love the kiddie Porsche. Yet she's miserable inside about the lime-green chiffon Rogue designed for her. It might be sex and the city for Sarah Jessica Parker, but Tweetie feels like Kermit the frog.

She's a brick about the Hunt Ball

The Good Sort

YOU CAN RELY on Lavinia. She organised the coaches to take the village to the Liberty and Livelihood March, and booked the MFH a table for breakfast at the Ritz. 'We can't march on an empty stomach,' she said. She walked so briskly that she went round twice, took several stiff gins off chums in Brooks's while pounding down St James's, then had an early lunch with a god-daughter bound for far-away places on her gap year. 'Never really cared for abroad myself, far too much to do at home, but here's £100 and don't stand any nonsense from the local tribesmen.'

She's a brick about the Hunt Ball. 'Of course you can have it at Doddington, the old place needs a bit of life. We can seat 50 for dinner and bung a marquee over the sunken garden for the gilded youth. All I ask is no stilettos – Tudor floors can't stand 'em.' Lavinia herself wears a trusty pair of Rayne court shoes, bought in 1972 and still perfectly good, and a dress flamboyantly impervious to fashion. She doesn't do clothes, wearing her late husband's shirts as night-dresses and stout tweed trousers from the Edinburgh Woollen Mill, although she was chuffed to bits with a pair of leopardette welling-tons given to her by her daughter. 'I say, how very splendid, the dogs won't know what to think if we go walkies in these tart traps.' They were certainly a vibrant talking point when she wore them to call the bingo numbers at the old-age pensioners' tea in the Memorial Hall. Lavinia's fashion moment was when the Duchess gave a fancy dress ball. Of course, she had a house party – 'Send along a dozen, no one too precious, the bathroom situation here's a bit creaky but I'll air the beds' – and appeared in a sari, legacy of a family vicere-ine. She also dug a very decent diamond medal out of the dressing-up box. 'Never keep anything in the safe – first place burglars look. It says decorations will be worn. I think this was Granny Sybil's.'

The Woman Who
Lives in Bed

WHY GET UP when you can stay in bed? In her formative years Venetia read that Lady Diana Cooper never rose until she had read *The Times* and dealt with her correspondence, an ideal role model from which no argument has persuaded her to deviate. Her Filipina maid brings her coffee and wholemeal toast, and takes Boris (originally after Pasternak, but now distinctly au courant with the rise of naughty Mr Johnson) for his constitutional. Venetia then spends a blissful morning chat-chat-chatting to the great and the good. Such gossip to share with Carla: does Nigel know that Annabel has dumped Otto von Strump? 'Agony for her, relinquishing squillions – it's been said that his family spirited the Amber Room away from that railway siding – but Otto was grotto in bed. He used to pounce on her wearing his ancestral armour, dreadfully unwieldy and cold.' Venetia dashes off her thank you letters on very stiff cards (wincy writing paper is hopeless when pressed against monogrammed sheets).

Like Jacqueline Kennedy, Venetia has fresh linen sheets every day. She slips the bill to her husband's secretary while he is at the IMF conference. He travels a lot, the uncluttered peace of a Four Seasons hotel bed being more soothing than negotiating his way through the labyrinthine infrastructure of Venetia's books, her Roberts radio, handbag, Filofax, homeopathic remedies, invitations and laptop. 'Darling, do be careful. Boris has asked me to write a book review for the *Spectator*. No, Johnson, not the dog. And we're at Covent Garden with the Magans on Monday, and you haven't forgotten the American ambassador on Tuesday, have you?' Everyone says they don't know how Venetia does it. It's because she has a little nap in the afternoon.

Venetia spends a blissful morning propped up on her linen pillows,
chat-chat-chatting to the great and the good

*Of course she slept with Mick – who didn't? – but then she married
the lead guitarist of Psychedelic Crash*

The Sixties Rock Chick

COSIMA HAS EYELASHES that were personally stuck on by Mary Quant in 1968 and have seemingly remained ever since, gathering old mascara like facial carpet sweepers. Of course she slept with Mick – who didn't? – but then she married the lead guitarist of Psychedelic Crash and life went a bit hazy, man. Y'know how it was: the yogi maharishi stuff in India; the ganja mind expansion in Jamaica; and the soul-finding desert experience in Morocco until she got bored of always having sand in her knickers and ran off with a marquess's son who was opening a tagine restaurant in Bath. It didn't work, not least because the citizens of Bath didn't like men wearing kaftans, even if they were lords. Yet Cosima loved the countryside, happily reminiscent of her Irish childhood, and her house became an impromptu animal sanctuary, orphaned owls roosting in the four-poster.

When a journalist came on a mission to discover What Happened to the Hippie Muses, Cosima's pet goat ate his overcoat. The lord left with his Deep Purple LPs to run a hotel in St Lucia and Cosi married the local doctor, mistaking him for the vet. Drifting back to London, she had a comeback in a David Bowie film, became a vegetarian and started designing ethno-jewellery made from beads and telephone wires by African tribes. She would never, she says, drawing deeply on an organic cigarette, dream of having a facelift, which is why she has so much hair, to hide the scars. 'My face tells my story,' is what she told Michael Parkinson, having put haemorrhoid cream round her eyes – an old modelling trick. Cosima is so now, partying with Nicky Haslam, chilling with Stella and Madge. The young think she's seriously cool, since her clothes are vintage – they come from her attic. In her next movie she's playing Jade Jagger's mother.

All are piled into Daisy's room in a melange of sleeping bags and duvets

The Sleepover

DAISY REALLY, REALLY wanted to have a sleepover for her birthday. Her mother, heart sinking, suggested it would be much nicer to take all her friends to the cinema, grasping desperately at the latest Leonardo DiCaprio movie. 'Or ice skating, darling?' Daisy just rolled her eyes. 'Mum, get real. I can't skate. Why would I want to spend my birthday falling over?' So a sleepover it is, and Daisy has invited Poppy, Georgie, Savannah, Caitlin and India. They are going to eat crisps, trash Daisy's older sister's make-up and watch MTV until 4am. Caitlin is well pleased because she's not allowed to eat crisps at home. Her mummy rang Daisy's mummy and said she wasn't to have any e-numbers. 'And may I recommend, Claire, that you do something with the girls so they don't just watch television. When Caitlin had a sleepover I got them all to make their own pizzas with healthy wholemeal dough. Such fun.' It's also why nobody will ever go to Caitlin's for a sleepover again. Claire has sensibly taken the line of least resistance – Pizza Express, which every schoolgirl knows is where real pizzas come from – and given up trying to get anyone to sleep in her charming spare bedrooms.

All are piled into Daisy's room in a melange of sleeping bags and duvets which, as the night wears on, crackle with discarded Celebrations wrappers and biscuit crumbs. There is high-octane giggling (re-runs of *Sex and the City* – about which Caitlin's mother will have words later), and noisy dancing to Britney. At one in the morning they all galumph down the stairs, squealing with over-excitement, to make toast and get more Diet Cokes out of the fridge. Then Savannah is sick, bursts into tears, and wants to go home, so has to be driven back to Clapham by Daisy's father who's had three whiskies and is furious that because his house is full of pre-teens he cannot watch the Fantasy Channel.

The Second-hand Shopper

EVERYONE SAYS SELINA looks absolutely marvellous, so unfair 'because she hasn't got a bean, you know'. They flog up and down Bond Street and come home with a series of heartbreaking fashion disasters, then Selina skips in wearing a little bit of vintage Chanel she picked up in the Marais. 'Darling, you are so sweet to notice, it was 30 francs from this heavenly little shop – I'll give you the address.' But she never does. Selina had Voyage cardies before Voyage; they were appliquéd by old Nanny. Selina feels Nanny really benefits from having something to do now she's nearly blind. Nanny lives in sheltered accommodation in Malmesbury, her sitting-room largely filled with bags of beads and pearls with which she is slowly and painfully embellishing Selina's shoes. It is a transformation the like of which has not been seen since Cinderella's slippers. Selina always buys her shoes in a back street in Florence. 'I can never do euros, but they're really cheap, wonderful shapes, and Nan does the magic.'

She smiles her secret smile, and swings the ocelot coat she found in an Oxfam shop near Cirencester for £10. Her friends are left chewing their Emma Hopes. 'If only I had the time I'd be able to find couture gems in the Portobello market too.' They say 'Oh my God, is that a real Kelly bag?' Selina bought it at auction at Christie's South Ken – '£50, the bliss' – on a horribly wet day when nobody else could find a taxi. Selina went on the bus. She loves bags: only Selina could have found a crocodile clutch in stinky Second Hand Rose which had a diamond brooch hidden in the lining. Some old duck must have tucked it away against burglars. Selina, sparkling with the diamonds which she's cleaned with vodka and a tooth-brush, can make quite a story of it. One day her wardrobe will be sold at Christie's – so amusing, so *Vogue* – and Selina will then have lots of beans.

*Selina skips in wearing a little bit of vintage Chanel she picked up
in the Marais*

Mossy is thinking of diversifying into bags, but her feather prototype looked like a moulting Pekingese

The Christmas Fair
Stallholder

IT WAS WHEN Mossy Dougdale put some cockerel feathers on to an old Alice band and wore them to a wedding, and everyone said how original she was, that Titfer Tat was born. Now it's quite a little business, and such fun setting up her stall at all the fairs in aid of asthma research, Macmillan Nurses, and the NSPCC. She's made lots of new friends; there's Patricia who bakes Aga cakes, Martha who sells ceramic noodle bowls, and Sally has done awfully well this year with sequinned coasters in the shape of pansies. The preview evening at the Christmas Spirit Fair heaved with American bankers' wives buying electronic wasp-zappers in the shape of little tennis rackets – 'Perfect. Hank loves killing things and he can't stand bugs' – and exploding golf balls. Mossy did rather well with her necklaces, a new line of semi-precious stones threaded on silver wire, for the bankers' daughters' stockings.

Mossy really prefers the country fairs. All her chums come to the one in Hampshire, it's rather a party and her velvet appliqué scarves do so well. Up in Yorkshire she stays with the Martins, they have a jolly dinner party, and as the evening wedding – the sartorial church-to-dance nightmare – has just arrived in the north Titfer Tat confections are much in demand. Mossy is thinking of diversifying into matching bags, but her feathery prototype looked like a moulting Pekingese. The baskets have done well, but then they are a Christmas fair staple, Mossy's inspiration was to line hers with gingham while watching *Changing Rooms*. She's not sure about the earrings. Her husband says they make her look like a Masai woman. 'Well, Hugo,' she said, 'you may laugh, but if it wasn't for me reinventing the Alice band we couldn't afford the repairs to the roof.'

The Book Club

JEANNINE IS SAYING that *The Catcher in the Rye* holds within its nexus the psychological meaning of adolescence. When she was growing up in New Jersey, JD Salinger was the touchstone of the tumultuous emotion of youth. Emily, Katie and Louisa are enraged by this bollocks; Emily's daughter Rose, passing through the kitchen on her way to China White, says she thinks it's completely saddo that a bunch of middle-aged women should be reading *The Catcher in the Rye* anyway. 'Hey, we all did that when we were 13 – where were you guys?' Emily feels all frail because she went to the sort of school where they gave prizes for hamster-keeping, and Katie gets wobbly because she didn't go to university. That's why she formed the Book Club, a sorority where everyone could eat comfort food around the kitchen table and talk about Dickens with their mouths full.

Then Jeannine muscled in, because she had limpetted on to Georgina, who did a themed Indian dinner when they all read *The God of Small Things* and felt sorry for Jeannine because she was American. Jeannine said, as they were reading *Birdsong* next month, she knew Sebastian Faulks and wouldn't it be marvellous if he could come along? All 11 other members of the Book Club recoil as if struck by cobras. A man! And worse, an author. What would they have to say to him? (One of the 12 chooses a book each month, and the chooser gives dinner.) Everyone adores Katie because she chose *The Pursuit of Love* and cooked Nigella's Blakeian fish pie. Jeannine chose *Memoirs of a Geisha* and served Evian and tiny sushi made by her Japanese chef. She told everyone they had to be moronic not to like the book. 'I am sure, like me, you've studied the author's background on the internet. Shouldn't we now progress to study Jewish writers?' But it's Emily's turn next and she's shamelessly chosen Jilly Cooper's *Pandora*.

A sorority where everyone can eat comfort food around the kitchen table and talk about Dickens

How was Chloe to know that Tony Blair was going to turn out to be a smug, sanctimonious little squit?

The Countryside
Campaigner

CHLOE IS A closet green wellie. Since she designs shoes with tiny, tiny heels like toothpicks, there were those surprised to see her on the march. 'Chloe! Good God, what are you wearing on your feet? Splendid, splendid – come and have a swift one at the Turf. I had you down as an anti.' Chloe is rather miffed, since she has just designed the most marvellous handbags with hounds picked out in sequins to go with foxy evening slippers for Knightsbridge/Gloucestershire weekend woman. She says, rather sniffily, that many people didn't know that David Hockney supported the Countryside Alliance.

Chloe has guilt. She voted for Tony Blair in 1997. How was she to know that he was going to turn out to be a smug, sanctimonious little squit? He reminds her of the boy who sneaked on everyone for smoking when she was in the sixth-form at Marlborough. If there's one thing Chloe can't stand, it's being told she can't do something. She may have achieved fashion celeb status, she may sell wispy sandals in Bergdorf Goodman, but her beating heart is at home with the Aga in Yorkshire. She used to walk hound puppies as a child. Now the pack may have to be destroyed and old Joe the huntsman will be out of work. Her friend the conceptual artist has told her she's a sentimental old thing, and Chloe says yes, she is, and proud of it. He may think it's sad to be reactionary at 25, but Chloe says it's new revolutionary, and she saw a Turner Prize artist next to Uncle Damien's terrier man on the march. It was such fun, particularly the couple mooning from a bedroom window at the Ritz. Chloe nipped in to go to the loo, and darling Michael Bentley, who's known Mummy for ever, was putting out crystal bowls of water for marching dogs. In weird times, this seems so comforting. Chloe now wants Nicholas Soames to be prime minister.

The Veteran Tennis Player

UNDERNEATH PATRICK'S BENEVOLENT exterior lurks a competitive demon. Only the vestigial influence of Nanny's disciplinary regime saves him from hideous outbursts à la John McEnroe – unattractive in a man of 65. As it is, if Patrick misses a ball he confines himself to a tight-lipped remonstration to his partner: 'Didn't you hear me say "Yours", old boy?' Opponents are distracted by the sight of his bushy eyebrows waggling over the net, whence he pops up to deliver a vicious drop volley. He particularly likes playing on his own court because he knows precisely where to ping the ball into the potholes so it bounces sideways.

As the passing years wreak havoc with his knees, Patrick recruits a succession of lithe young things – the sparky blonde friends of his daughters – to run around the court while he stands on the baseline, whipping back the forehands. 'Come over and let's knock up, we'll have a friendly and then some serious Pimm's.' Anyone deluded by this insouciance will be beaten to a pulp and hung out to dry. New neighbours are favourite prey. They turn up in new Nikes, carrying bunches of graphite Thundersticks. 'Only sad my Maxply gave out, terrific weapon,' says Patrick, with a tigerish smile, plaque Slazenger-yellow. The neighbours talk nervously about how well they did in the round robin at the Harbour Club, only to find themselves one set down socially. They fall on the Pimm's gasping about hay fever, off days and bad backs, and how Patrick must come over and play on their new Grassovelvet all-weather surface court. He will, but first there is his old school's veterans match, a highlight of the year. Through to the semi-finals, he wakes shuddering with the most terrific nightmare, to be calmly reassured by his wife from the depths of her Dorothy Sayers: 'Don't worry, Patrick, it's 40-love and you are serving.'

Anyone deluded by Patrick's insouciance will be beaten to a pulp and hung out to dry

The Elvis Impersonator

ERIC IS EXHAUSTED. The 25th anniversary of the King's death has almost been too much. After the hen night in Penge, the rock'n'roll extravaganza in Stoke Newington and the Elvis convention in Torre del Mar, he would have given anything to be able to book into the Heartbreak Hotel. Sometimes, teasing his quiff in the mirror, Eric-Elvis feels he doesn't know who he is any more. It has been a long journey from Solihull to Memphis. It was his mam, Maisie, who'd done some of her most memorable snogging to *Love Me Tender*, who spotted that her Eric had an Elvis mouth. 'It must be wish fulfilment, duck, give you a bit of spangle and you could be him.' Fortunately, with a microphone, singing lessons, backing tape and the enhancing environs of smoky clubs with no acoustics, Eric could sing. His fame spread in Solihull. Women at the Kitty Kat Klub threw their knickers at him. Eric perfected the hip wiggle that brought 100 women from the Women's Institute to their feet, hollering and weeping. He then perfected the art of wiping his sweating brow, after *Hound Dog*, with a red polyester scarf covered in gold musical notes and handing it out to the more clamorous middle-aged fans wobbling in Lycra at the stage's edge.

Eric has since had the Elvis nose job – his gig in Rotterdam paid for that – and a little wig, tucked in under the quiff, which is now dyed. Dying his chest hair is truly weird, but what can a serious Elvis do? He now holds his stomach in with a rhinestone belt, as if he had indeed been eating multiple peanut butter and jelly sandwiches with burgers on rye to follow. His skin is orange with panstick, and he has to wear sunglasses because his eyes, pinky and weepy, still look more Solihull than Elvis. He and Priscilla, his living doll, are going to Memphis for their honeymoon.